A PICTURE BOOK OF
HARRY HOUDINI

by David A. Adler and Michael S. Adler
illustrated by Matt Collins

Holiday House / New York

To Amy
—M. C.

Text copyright © 2009 by David A. Adler and Michael S. Adler
Illustrations copyright © 2009 by Matt Collins
All Rights Reserved
HOLIDAY HOUSE is registered in the U. S. Patent and Trademark Office.
Printed and Bound in February 2010 at Tien Wah Press, Johor Bahru, Johor, Malaysia
www.holidayhouse.com

3 5 7 9 10 8 6 4 2

Library of Congress Cataloging-in-Publication Data
Adler, David A.
A picture book of Harry Houdini / by David A. Adler and Michael S. Adler ; illustrated by Matt Collins.
— 1st ed.
p. cm.
ISBN 978-0-8234-2059-9 (hardcover)
1. Houdini, Harry, 1874-1926—Juvenile literature.
2. Magicians—United States—Biography—Juvenile literature.
3. Magicians—United States—Pictorial works—Juvenile literature.
4. Escape artists—United States—Biography—Juvenile literature.
5. Escape artists—United States—Pictorial works—Juvenile literature.
I. Adler, Michael S. II. Collins, Matt, ill. III. Title.
GV1545.H8A5 2009
793.8092—dc22
[B]
2008023212
ISBN 978-0-8234-2302-6 (paperback)

Two men lifted the great Harry Houdini and lowered him into a large water-filled can.

"If I fail to appear," Houdini told his audience, "my assistants will do everything possible to save my life."

Houdini ducked under the water. The men sealed the can with a metal lid and secured it with six heavy metal padlocks. The curtain closed.

One minute passed, then two, then three. The audience was tense. They were sure no one could survive so long underwater. Finally, the curtain opened. A very wet Harry Houdini stepped forward and bowed. The metal can was behind him, still locked.

This was just one of many escapes Houdini made during his career. He freed himself from ropes, handcuffs, straitjackets, and prison cells. He was the most celebrated escape artist and magician of his time.

Harry Houdini was born on March 24, 1874, in Budapest, Hungary. He was named Ehrich by his parents, Rabbi Mayer Samuel and Cecilia Weisz. He was one of their six children. Shortly after Ehrich was born, his father changed the spelling of the family name to Weiss and moved his family to Appleton, Wisconsin. There Ehrich's father became rabbi of the town's new synagogue.

Rabbi Weiss, who never learned English, soon lost his job. The family moved to Milwaukee, where Rabbi Weiss gave Hebrew lessons. Work for him was scarce, so young Ehrich helped out by selling newspapers and shining shoes.

When traveling circuses came to town, Ehrich watched the magicians. He tried to perform their tricks. At age nine he got a job in a "five-cent" circus. He wore long red stockings and called himself "the Prince of the Air."

At eleven he took a job with the local locksmith. There he often played with the locks and soon could open them all without keys. He used pins and pieces of bent wire.

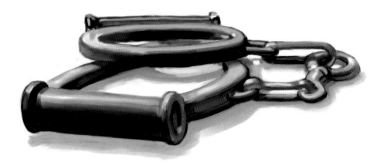

When he was twelve, Ehrich ran away from home. He wandered, did odd jobs, and performed magic whenever he could. For a time he joined a circus as an escape artist. He called himself "Eric the Great."

In 1887 the Weiss family moved to New York City, where Ehrich's father hoped he could find work. Ehrich joined them. There he worked as a department store messenger, photographer's assistant, and necktie cutter. But his passion was magic.

Ehrich read a book, *Memoirs of Robert-Houdin*, a nineteenth-century French magician. In 1891 Ehrich changed his first name to Harry, after Harry Kellar, a popular American magician, and his family name from Weiss to Houdini. The added "i" at the end meant "like Houdin."

Early in 1894 Harry met Beatrice "Bess" Raymond, a singer and dancer. They fell in love and married on July 22, 1894.

Bess took care of her husband. When he performed, she was often onstage as his assistant. She described her husband as "the most helpless man in the world."

Once when Bess couldn't travel with him, she packed for his trip and labeled each shirt so Houdini would know when to wear it. It didn't help. When he returned home, all the shirts were still in his bag, still labeled. He had worn the same shirt all week.

At first Houdini's act was rather ordinary. He did card tricks and pulled a handkerchief through a tube and it changed colors. But then he added escape tricks and attracted lots of attention.

In each town Houdini visited, he went to the police station and asked to be locked up. He quickly freed himself. Newspaper stories of his escapes brought people to his shows.

In May 1900 Houdini and his wife sailed to England. There he challenged the famed British police of Scotland Yard to handcuff him. They locked his hands, sure he couldn't get loose. But he did.

In Germany special cuffs were made to hold him, but they couldn't. And the theaters in England, Germany, France, and Russia couldn't hold all the people who wanted to see his shows.

In 1904 when the Houdinis returned to America, Harry was an international star.

In 1907 Houdini performed his first bridge jump. He was locked in chains, then he jumped off a Rochester, New York, bridge into the icy water below. He soon emerged unchained and unharmed.

On July 7, 1912, Houdini performed one of his most dangerous escapes. He climbed inside a coffin that was then nailed shut, tied with ropes and steel bands, and thrown into the water off New York's Governors Island. In less than one minute Houdini was free.

This trick was big news. People were anxious to see him do it again, so a huge water tank was put on a stage in a New York theater. Night after night Houdini was locked in a box that was thrown into the water, and night after night he broke free.

On January 7, 1918, in one of his greatest illusions, Houdini made a 10,000-pound elephant and her trainer disappear from a wooden cabinet. "The matinee crowds will worry themselves into sleep," a newspaper reviewer noted, "wondering what Houdini did with his elephant."

Houdini refused to disappoint his audiences. Once, while performing, he broke his ankle. Still, he insisted on finishing the show.

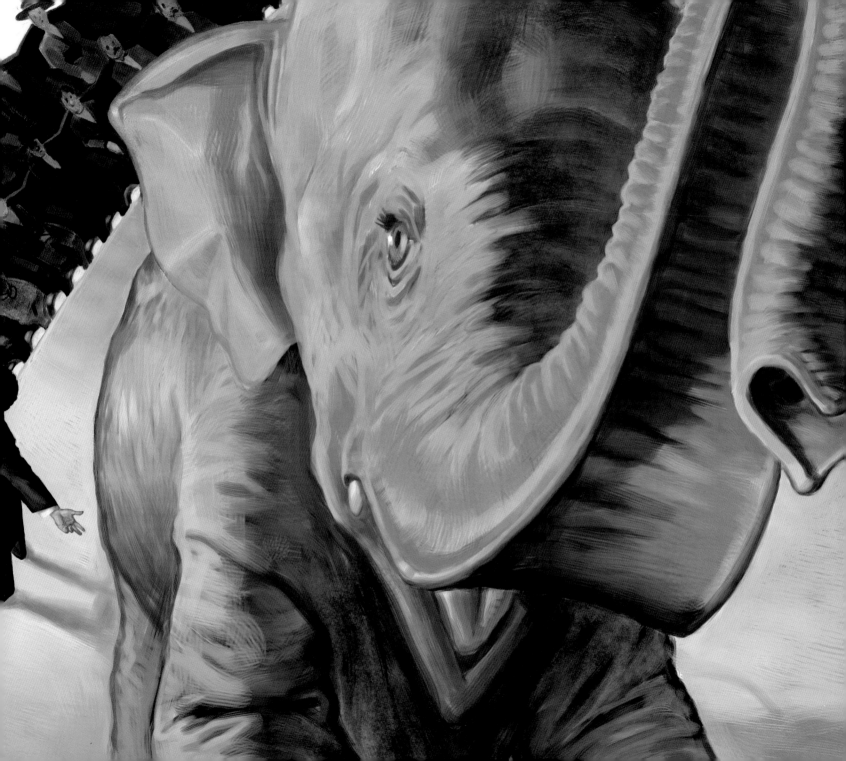

During World War I Houdini gave free shows for American soldiers. At one show he pulled an eagle out of a flag. He also pulled gold coins from the air and threw them to the soldiers as keepsakes.

In 1913 Cecilia Weiss, Houdini's mother, died. Houdini missed her greatly; and hoping to reconnect with her, he visited spiritualists, people who said they could speak to the dead. Everyone he met was a fake and their trickery upset him. He exposed them, often from the stage as part of his act.

On October 22, 1926, Houdini was in Montreal, Canada. Some students came to his dressing room and asked if it was true that he was so strong, he could take a punch without being hurt. Houdini said it was true. Then, before he could tighten his stomach muscles, one student punched him a few times. Houdini fell.

Houdini was severely injured but still performed that day and the next. But on October 24, 1926, he collapsed. The blows to his stomach had ruptured his appendix, which became inflamed and infected.

A few days later, lying on a hospital bed, he whispered, "I am tired of fighting. Guess this thing is going to get me."

On October 31, 1926, Harry Houdini died. His body was sent home to New York City. On November 4, 1926, more than two thousand people attended his funeral.

"He was exceptional, a unique personality," the rabbi said at the service, "and besides that, he was one of the noblest and sweetest of men."

IMPORTANT DATES

1874 Born Ehrich Weisz in Budapest, Hungary, March 24.

1883 Makes professional debut in Jack Hoeffle's Five-Cent Circus.

1891 Changes his name from Ehrich Weiss to Harry Houdini.

1894 Marries Beatrice "Bess" Raymond, July 22.

1900 Travels to Europe and performs there.

1904 Returns to America.

1906 Escapes the Washington, D.C., prison cell that once held Charles J. Guiteau, the assassin of President James A. Garfield, January 6.

1908 Performs famed milk can escape, January 27.

1912 Escapes from coffin while submerged in water just off Governors Island, New York, July 7.

1918 Makes a 10,000-pound elephant and her trainer vanish, January 7.

1926 Dies from appendicitis, October 31.

SOURCE NOTES

Each source note includes the first word or words and the last word or words of a quotation and its source. References are to books cited in the Selected Bibliography.

"If I fail . . . my life.": Gresham, p. 137.
"the most . . . in the world.": Woog, p. 87.
"The matinee . . . with his elephant." Christopher, p. 154.

"I am tired . . . get me.": Gresham, pp. 244–245.

"He was . . . sweetest of men.": Christopher, p. 262.

SELECTED BIBLIOGRAPHY

Christopher, Milbourne. *Houdini: The Untold Story.* New York: Pocket Books, 1969.

Gibson, Walter B., and N. Morris Young, eds. *Houdini on Magic.* New York: Dover Publications, 1953.

Gresham, William Lindsay. *Houdini: The Man Who Walked Through Walls.* New York: Holt, Rinehart and Winston, 1959.

"Harry Houdini Dies After Operations." *New York Times,* November 1, 1926 (reprinted www.nytimes.com/learning/general/onthisday/bday/0324.html).

Kellock, Harold. *Houdini: His Life-Story.* New York: Blue Ribbon Books, 1928.

Williams, Beryl, and Samuel Epstein. *The Great Houdini.* New York: Pocket Books, 1951.

Woog, Adam. *The Importance of Harry Houdini.* San Diego: Lucent Books, 1995.

RECOMMENDED WEBSITES

www.pbs.org/wgbh/amex/houdini/

www.americaslibrary.gov/cgi-bin/page.cgi/aa/houdini

www.magictricks.com/houdini/bio.htm

www.nytimes.com/learning/general/onthisday/bday/0324.html

AUTHORS' NOTES

While Houdini claimed to have been born in America, research performed after his death uncovered his Hungarian birth certificate. Houdini's birth date has also been the subject of dispute, as many, including his mother, placed it as April 6, 1874; but his birth certificate lists it as March 24, 1874.

Bess Houdini often said, "I am the most married person I know, three times, and to the same man!" The first ceremony was civil, followed by one before a rabbi; and because Bess was Catholic, they were married a third time by a priest.

Houdini was close with his mother, and after her death on July 17, 1913, he canceled his shows for a month. Those who knew him said he was not the same after that.

In February 1926 Houdini went before Congress in support of a law that would have banned fortune-telling in Washington, D.C. It did not pass.

Harry Houdini was buried with a packet of his mother's letters beneath his head.